Jump and Shout

CHEERLEADING GEAR

TRACY NELSON MAURER

Rourke
Publishing LLC
Vero Beach, Florida 32964

Project Assistance courtesy of Jennifer Tell, Dance and Cheer Factory, Forest Lake, Minnesota.

The author also extends appreciation to Mike Maurer, Kendall and Lois Nelson, the Rourke team, Tammy Tonn, Melissa Martyr-Wagner, Princeton University, and the University of Minnesota Alumni Association.

Photo Credits: Cover, pgs p12, 16, 27, 28, 31 ©Peter Schlitt/PHOTOSPORT.COM
Title, pgs 4, 9, 10, 11, 17, 18, 19, 24 ©PHOTOSPORT.COM
pgs 14, 15, 20, 21, 23, 35, 36, 44 ©PIR
pg 6 from the Library of Congress
pg 34 ©USDA/Ken Hammond
p40 ©Paul Martinez/PHOTOSPORT.COM

Editor: Frank Sloan

Cover and page design: Nicola Stratford

Notice: This book contains information that is true, complete, and accurate to the best of our knowledge. However, the author and Rourke Publishing LLC offer all recommendations and suggestions without any guarantees and disclaim all liability incurred in connection with the use of this information.

Safety first! Activities appearing or described in this publication may be dangerous. Always work with a trained coach and spotters when learning new cheerleading skills.

Library of Congress Cataloging-in-Publication Data

Maurer, Tracy, 1965-
  Cheerleading gear / Tracy Nelson Maurer.
     p. cm. -- (Jump and shout)
  Summary: "Cheerleaders blend amazing athletic skills and spirited talent to perform breathtaking stunts. They work hard to boost school pride and win over judges at stiff competitions. Coaches expect teamwork, dedication, good grades, and healthy attitudes"--Provided by publisher.
  Includes index.
  ISBN 1-59515-502-3 (hardcover)
  1. Cheerleading--Juvenile literature. I. Title. II. Series.
  LB3635.M26 2006
  791.6'4--dc22
                              2005012716

Printed in the USA

cg/cg

Rourke Publishing
1-800-394-7055
www.rourkepublishing.com
sales@rourkepublishing.com
Post Office Box 3328, Vero Beach, FL 32964

TABLE OF CONTENTS

A young cheerleader is off to a good start!

Chapter 1

Have you watched little boys and girls play with cheerleading **pompons**? They wildly shake the stringy poufs for as much noise as they can muster. Kids swing the pompons over their heads. They toss them into the air. They smile, and you can't help smiling with them.

Were you ever like one of those kids? Some people never outgrow that pompon magic. They crave cheerleading's excitement, the noise, and the opportunity to share their **enthusiasm**. The uniform, gear, equipment, and gadgets galore add to the experience. But cheerleading's history started long before pompons.

Ancient Cheers?

Nobody knows for sure when people started cheering. Many ancient civilizations from the Mayans to the Chinese played sports and held public competitions. Research shows that large groups of people watched the contests.

Did they yell or sing during the competitions? Did they clap? Did they rattle drums or shake noisemakers? Maybe they danced or **gestured** to show their enthusiasm. Perhaps they prayed. Many events had religious ties, and some "games" ended with brutal sacrifices.

Can you imagine *quiet* spectators at the chariot races, wrestling matches, or marathons in ancient Greece? Records from early Olympic events suggest that crowds doted on their favorite athletes. They praised achievement and skill.

Public announcements shamed any cheaters. A guilty athlete paid a fine, which was used to make a small gold statue. The athlete's name and his blunder were inscribed on the statue. These statues lined the roadways to the games like billboards.

Greek Policy

The Greeks defined sportsmanship. Many code-of-conduct policies for today's athletes borrow from the Greek ideals of fair play.

Even in ancient times, fans cheered on their favorite athletes.

Won by a Thumb

Crowd power grew under the sly ancient Roman emperors. The leaders designed pageants and bloody "games" as entertainment to keep citizens too busy to overthrow the government.

It worked for decades. People flocked to Rome's 50,000-seat Colosseum and other huge sports venues to watch the deadly gladiator battles and participate in the crowd "voting."

The audience often decided the competition results—and the gladiators' fates. An injured gladiator could ask for the crowd's mercy. The fans would either gesture "thumbs-up" to pardon his life and grant his freedom, or they showed "thumbs-down" to call for his execution.

Thanks to cheerleaders, today's crowds can still influence the game's outcome—but in far less gory ways than the early Romans.

Thumbs Up

One of the earliest known crowd gestures, thumbs-up still shows approval. Fans everywhere raise their thumbs to cheer for their favorite athletes and teams.

All Together Now

Crowds have played an important role in sports events for centuries, but organized cheering didn't start until the late 1800s.

Historians say cheerleading officially began in 1889 when Johnny "Jack" Campbell stood before University of Minnesota football fans and encouraged them to yell poem-like verses in **unison** to show support for the team:

"Rah, Rah, Rah! Ski-u-mah! Hoo-rah! Hoo-rah! Varsity! Varsity! Minn-e-so-tah!"

Before Campbell's leadership, individual voices from the stands had sounded like babble down on the football field. All together, the fans sounded big, loud, and proud. The players heard the crowd and won the game.

Cheerleading quickly became popular at schools across the country. All-male "yell squads" or "pep clubs" boosted school spirit with simple **chants** and rhymes. The guys sang school songs, or **rousers**, with their school bands. They focused on revving up the athletes, not performing.

All-male pep squads gave way to co-ed groups.

Mega Noise

Not long before Johnny Campbell needed a tool to help yell to the crowd, Thomas Edison invented the **telephonoscope** as a personal hearing aid. An excited *New York Herald* reporter called it a **"megaphone"** in 1878.

Megaphone eventually came to mean a long, funnel-shaped device used to **amplify** and direct sound. It works on the same principle as cupping your hands to your mouth and yelling. The megaphone's horn increases sound pressure levels, or volume. Sound waves carry further.

Megaphones have been popular with cheerleaders since the beginning.

Cheerleading's First Symbol

Edison used a similar cone-shaped speaker on his amazing phonograph invention, but he didn't actually invent the cheerleading megaphone. Nobody knows who did—the simple design goes too far back in history. Edison's name, however, stayed connected with the gadget when cheerleading first gained popularity in the early 1900s.

Edison's worldwide fame probably helped make the megaphone trendy with college crowds. Movie directors called "Action!" through megaphones, and famous singers like Rudy Vallee then adopted the device in their acts, too. Megaphones gave early cheerleaders a hip, cool look.

Megaphones showed up in trendy Hollywood advertisements.

Even today, cheerleaders sometimes use megaphones. Many squads have replaced their traditional brass yelling cones with louder electronic models. Still, cheerleading's first gadget became its **icon**, or symbol.

Megaphones amplify a cheer.

Chapter 2

PERFORMANCE

OUTFITS

Unlike early pep squads, today's cheerleaders—male and female—do more than simply lead cheers. They nail stunts with big-air jumps. They flip through breathtaking **tumbling runs.** They dance. *They perform.*

Cheerleaders wear dazzling uniforms and use flashy props to add excitement to the **choreography**.

If you join a cheerleading squad, your outfit—or outfits— might depend on the team's focus and where you live.

Cheerleaders, like all other athletes, need uniforms that allow them to move freely. Baggy tops and bottoms feel heavy and binding. They look sloppy. Coaches prefer teams to wear stretchy fabrics that fit snugly without pinching or creeping into unsightly places.

Generally, girls wear fitted tops and thigh-high skirts over bloomers or briefs (cover-ups for your panties) or they wear skorts, skirts with built-in shorts. Sometimes they wear jazzy shorts. Guys wear fitted shirts and long pants, shorts, or jams—long shorts.

Athletic Style

Today's uniforms reflect fashion trends more closely than ever, especially for competition cheerleading teams. Tops and bottoms catch attention with sequins, cutouts, and metallic accents. Outfits might match a theme or music. Contest costumes dare to show some skin, especially a toned tummy, back, or shoulders.

Short tops are comfortable and fashionable.

14

Stunts demonstrate the athletic ability of today's cheerleaders.

Schools tend to shy away from outfits that reveal too much. School cheerleaders usually wear uniforms in the team colors. Back in the 1950s when cheerleading uniforms became popular, the girls often wore "letter sweaters" over long wool skirts. The letters stood for the school name, such as CHS for Central High School. Some squads still use letters, but most feature a **mascot** or symbol.

Tuck In at Tryouts

Tuck in your shirt at tryouts, even if you think it's dweeby. You'll look neater and more serious. Untucked is also unsafe.

15

Uniforms are designed with school colors in mind.

What a Drag!

The first female cheerleaders joined the University of Minnesota squads in the 1920s. Those peppy ladies dressed in heavy wool sweaters and ankle-length skirts, but they managed to introduce tumbling moves to cheerleading.

Weather Worries

If you live in a northern state, your coach considers the weather when selecting uniforms. Fall temperatures often dip below 32°F (0°C) during evening football games. Your uniform might include sweaters, hats, mittens, and legwarmers.

Even in the cold, your cheerleading jumps and moves can make you sweaty. Try adding a thin fabric T-shirt under your sweater to wick moisture away from your body.

If you live in a southern state where the sun can bake the football field to a toasty 100°F (37°C) or higher, your coach wants the team to stay cool. The coach might select lightweight, breathable fabrics that wick away moisture. Heat exhaustion can make you sick. It can kill, too.

Uniforms of the past were a bit more plain than today's fashions.

Long bottoms keep cheerleaders warm on the ice.

Whatever uniform your team wears, take care of it. Read the instructions or show the label to the person who usually does your laundry. Sweaty uniforms need immediate washing. Normally, you hand wash and line dry (not dry clean) your cheerleading outfit.

Professional cheerleaders usually have several different outfits, but they are all attention getters.

Pro Glamour

The Baltimore Colts welcomed the first professional cheerleading squad in 1960. Sixteen years later, the Dallas Cowboys cheerleaders stirred up the crowds with their stunning outfits and glamorous style.

Stand for Quality

Your team may have a competition costume and a game uniform. You might also have a team warm-up suit and special cheerleading camp clothes. Your coach might require running-style shorts and tucked-in T-shirts at tryouts and practices.

Some coaches select team shoes, but many simply set guidelines for shoes that fit well and look good. Your feet take a pounding as you stomp, jump, and stunt. Even standing on the sidelines puts pressure on your feet.

Think about how you'll use (and abuse) your shoes. Will you cheer indoors? Outdoors? Both?

Just like marathon runners choose shoes built for running, look for shoes made for cheerleading. Almost all cheerleading shoes offer lightweight, well-cushioned designs with team-colored inserts to dress up basic white.

Shoes should be clean, comfortable, and durable.

Some cheerleading shoes feature finger grips or grooves that help with stunts and tumbling. You absolutely need snug stability and solid traction, especially for stunts. **Bases** must hold their feet steady to balance the **flyer**. Flyers must climb on the bases. Their shoes shouldn't scratch or gouge.

Try on the shoes for fit and feel. Ankle and arch support, durability, flexibility, shock absorption, and **ventilation** vary. Comfort matters! You'll spend countless hours wearing the shoes at practices and performances.

Figure on spending between $30 and $70 on shoes. Quality costs more. Don't skimp. Shoes complete your uniform. They're also your personal safety equipment.

Under It All

Don't blush. What's under your uniform matters, too. Guys wear athletic supporters or jock straps. Look for soft, non-chafing fabrics that wick away moisture. Buy the right size, too.

Bloomers cover what your skirt can't.

Many guys layer a sweat-wicking T-shirt under the uniform top to prevent underarm puddles. Stock up on thirsty athletic socks that cushion your feet, too. Sweaty feet churn up more blisters (and more odor).

Girls should also wear thick, cushioned athletic socks, especially at practices. Many teams wear dance tights for performances. These often have built-in panties. No panty lines. No skivvies peaking out from your bloomers.

Finding the right bra is a bit trickier. Your comfort, support, and confidence depend on that rig.

Athletic bras usually feature more durable construction and less padding than your everyday bra. Racerbacks or T-backs are the most common styles. Underwires generally offer good support, while stretchy fabrics move with you.

If you're curvy, you need to minimize the bounce factor to reduce muscle strain. Even if you're petite on top, you want peek-proof coverage and moisture-wicking comfort. Take time to find the right fit and style.

Fit Right

Too tight? Too loose? A professional bra fitting at a department store can help you. Try before you buy.

Many uniforms are designed with pieces that can be mixed and matched.

A 1950s-era cheerleader shows off an early version of pompons.

Chapter 3

POMPON MAGIC

Of all the gear and gadgets cheerleaders use, pompons hold the most magic. They charm children and mesmerize cheerleaders-in-training. Those colorful balls of fluffy plastic strips command attention during chants—the short, repeated phrases yelled from the sidelines. Pompons also rustle up extra excitement during **cheers**—the longer routines performed for breaks in the game action or at competitions.

That's exactly why Lawrence Herkimer, often called the father of cheerleading, created modern pompons in 1956. He realized cheerleaders needed a bold, colorful prop to emphasize their hand gestures at a distance.

Herkimer also guessed that Americans would buy the newfangled color televisions just hitting the store shelves then. Camera crews already broadcast football games. He wanted the cheerleading teams to be more visible on TV screens.

Herkimer attached bright paper streamers to a stick. With a swish and a swoosh, he shook cheerleading performances to new heights. He and his wife opened a business to sell the fun cheerleading accessory. Soon cheerleaders everywhere added the prop to their halftime routines—if it wasn't raining. Water wilted the paper shakers.

Luckily, vinyl replaced paper pompons in 1968. Today, pompons have joined megaphones as cheerleading icons.

Pompons or Pompoms?

How do you spell them?
P-o-m-p-o-n-s.
That's the traditional and most proper spelling, honoring the word's French roots. But it's not the only accepted spelling. Different dictionaries list "pompoms," "pom-poms," and "pom-pons," too. A "pompom" actually refers to a cannon. However, "pompom girls" are not soldiers. They're performers who use pompons like cheerleaders do, but may or may not lead cheers. And people think cheerleading is simple. Sheesh!

POMPONS ADD PIZAZZ

27

s-sh-shh-shhh-Shake, Shake, Shake!

Pompons attract attention and accent your gestures through color, movement, and sound. Few props do so much so simply!

Even the youngest cheerleaders can shake pompons. How old were you when you held your first set? Some programs accept three-year-olds! Coaches often add pompons to performance routines for very young cheerleaders to make the kids more visible.

Pompons pump up the action in cheers with small stunts, too. At first, you'll work more with pompons than when you progress to more difficult cheers and stunts. Pompons get in the way when you try trickier moves.

If you're on a school cheerleading team, you'll use pompons at the games. Rustling pompons accent the beat and rhythm in cheers and chants like drums or other percussion instruments do.

Experiment! What do short, sharp, jabbing pompon motions sound like? Try sweeping fast figure-eights over your head. Or, slowly rumble the pompons by your knees, then tweak them faster and faster as you raise them up into the air. Toss and catch them. Mix in a few stomps. Pompons kick up your sideline and halftime choreography.

Pompon Variety

Many companies make and sell pompons today. You'll find pompons in any size, color, pattern, or style you can imagine! Catalogs and Web sites showcase poufs with sparkling metallic strands or flashing colored lights.

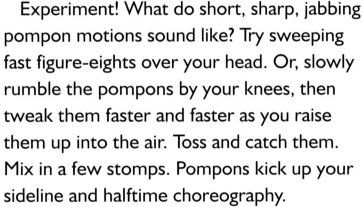

Colorful pompons grab the crowd's attention.

Some pompons fit on your hand with straps, and others hang from a dowel or stick-like handle. A baton handle, another option, connects two poufs, so your hand disappears inside the streamers.

Generally, cheerleaders use rooter pompons, show pompons, and specialty pompons. Your team might use one or several styles, depending on your focus.

Baton Handle

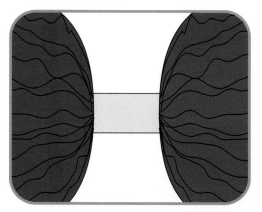
Dowel Handle

ROOTER POMPONS

Very young cheerleaders and fans in the stands like to wave these colorful tassels. Also called "shakers," rooter pompons have some 500 thin streamers measuring about 12 inches (30.5 cm) long clustered onto a stick-like handle. Cheerleaders often sell them at games for fundraisers.

SHOW POMPONS

Plumper than rooter pompons, the bushy cheer or show pompons range in diameter from 6 inches (15.2 cm) to 16 inches (40.6 cm). Streamer widths and handles vary, too. Competition teams usually custom-order show pompons to match their uniforms or to accent their routines.

Pompons add color, movement, and sound to a cheer.

SPECIALTY POMPONS

Specialty pompons include just about anything round and fluffy that shows your school pride. Hair pompons for ponytails and shoelace pompons complete your uniform. They also make fun fundraiser items.

Pamper Your Pompons

Many schools re-use their pompons for several years. If you luck out with a new set, expect your pompons to arrive flat. Follow the company's fluffing instructions. Usually, you crunch up the streamers in your hands over and over again. It takes time. Once they're plump, don't pile junk on your pompons in your locker or your room. They'll flatten or crease. Spills? Muddy splashes? Use mild soap and water to wash pompons. Always air dry wet pompons before you put them away. They'll stink if you don't!

Chapter 4

PRACTICE SAFETY

When you commit to a cheerleading squad, you promise to practice and perform your best. You agree to follow the team rules. Safety comes first.

As a teammate, you share responsibility for your squad's safety. Start by sleeping enough! If you're groggy, you lose focus, and that's when those major head-cracking injuries happen.

Eat a healthy diet, too. Your body gains strength from proper nutrition. Eating too much or not enough changes how your body performs—and that changes the team's performance.

A healthy diet is essential for good performance.

Physical fitness plays a larger part in cheerleading now than ever before. Big-air jumps and daring stunts demand limber, strong muscles for safe, precise performances. Conditioning your body lowers the risk of injuries.

Balanced **quadriceps** and **hamstring** muscles prevent **anterior cruciate ligament** (ACL) damage, for example. The ACL holds your knee steady and connects your thighbone to the shinbone. Females sprain and tear their ACLs more often than males. How bad is it? Forget cheerleading for the next six to nine months—if your ACL surgery and follow-up therapy go well. If not, you might be benched for good.

Fortunately, most cheerleading injuries are minor. Split lips, wrenched wrists, and jammed or twisted ankles top the list. It's not unusual to see teammates wearing a wrist, ankle, or knee brace during practices or performances.

Conditioning Gear

Your coach should develop practice sessions that include gentle warm-up exercises, stretching, strength training, and **cardiovascular** workouts. A safety-minded coach thinks about your age, athletic abilities, and cheerleading skills before starting the cheerleading conditioning program. Ask your coach for drills and exercises to do at home, too.

Every practice and every performance should begin with stretching exercises.

Many types of equipment help build your strength, flexibility, and **endurance**. In time, you might work with:

- Hand weights
- Stretchy resistance bands
- Weighted medicine balls
- Incline mats or "cheese" mats
- Large body balls

Yell cheers or chants while you jump rope or hula-hoop, too. Play music from your halftime show and dance. Have fun!

Safety Zones

Your team should learn proper spotting techniques and use extra spotters when trying new skills, especially more advanced moves. Spotters stop a flyer's head from whacking the ground. Spotting takes complete attention, quick thinking, and fast action. Know how!

A spotter may have the most important job on the team.

Like all athletes, you need a safe place to work out. Injuries happen most often at practices when you're learning new skills. Your practice facility should have high ceilings, fans or air conditioning, and proper mats.

Don't rely on the mats instead of your good judgment. If you're not ready to try a new move, stop. Take your time to work up to it. Mats will cushion your fall, but they won't take the pain out of a sprain.

Smart Cheering

Your high school's safety rules are probably much, much longer than this list. The official safety recommendations change with new research, too. Put safety first. That's smart cheering.

- ❁ Never practice stunts without your coach.
- ❁ No tumbling over, under, or through anything, including people or equipment.
- ❁ Forget the mini-trampoline.
- ❁ No flips or falls off of pyramids and shoulders.
- ❁ No stunts over two people high.

Chapter 5

MORE $TUFF

Scan any cheerleading magazine or Web site and your wallet whimpers. Companies across America sell oodles of gear, doodads, and equipment.

You can buy cheerleading pompons, uniforms, magazine subscriptions, video training tools, books, scrapbooking craft kits, drums, noisemakers, megaphones, sign-making kits, glow necklaces, beach balls, metallic streamers, face paint, sidewalk chalk, and window paints. You can sign up for camps and contests, too—some on cruise ships and in exotic tropical locations.

Chaaa-ching!

Cheerleading isn't cheap. Even if your school provides the uniform (about $100), you probably pay for your bloomers, socks, shoes, and other doodads—figure another $100. Many schools charge activity fees ranging from $50 to $125. Some squads require you to attend camp, too. That's maybe $250. You'll wear special camp clothing, of course, and that's another $75. Ouch!

Let your parents know what expenses you expect. And thank them often.

Funding Factors

School budgets rarely cover an entire cheerleading program. Some coaches receive salaries or **stipends** and maybe funds for safety training. Many coaches spend their own money and volunteer countless extra hours.

Activity fees at your school probably help with the costs of practice facilities, mats, workout gear, and transportation to games and competitions. Uniform costs, judging stipends, and contest and camp fees often pass onto the team.

Cheerleaders use their energy to organize fundraisers. Bake sales, car washes, and garage sales help cheerleaders bring in dollars. Some teams sell products or game programs, run concession stands, or trade for donations by making special appearances at business grand openings or other events.

What can you sell to make money for your team? Entire catalogs and Web sites feature merchandise for fund-raising programs. You'll see pompons, clickers, scented candles, popcorn, chocolates, pizzas, frozen sweet breads, and just about anything else!

You're Beautiful!

Real-life cheerleaders beam with an honest, fresh, fun, and all-American appearance that comes from dedication, hard work, and positive attitude.

Ignore the hype. Expensive makeup, hairstyle and goop, fad diets or diet pills, or even plastic surgery simply can't replace a beautiful personality.

Focus on fitness, not fatness. Zip any negative comments about your body shape or size—or anyone else's. As you practice, you'll tone and firm your body to its natural shape.

Picks for Your Pack

Makeup

Skin care does more for your looks than makeup. Cleanse and moisturize. Wear at least an SPF 15 sunscreen. Sometimes cheerleaders add extra eyeliner, cheek color, bronzing powder, or shine-control powder for performances. Go easy on the sparkles. You want to be seen—not create a scene.

Lips

Your lips can dry and crack in the sun and wind. Keep lip balm handy. Gals might wear noticeable lipgloss or lipstick to help the crowd see their smiles. If your parents approve, try a nice pink or rose lip color. Dark colors cast a creepy, back-from-the-dead image. Aaack!

Hair

Style your hair away from your face. Try side braids, French braids, or side ponytails. Some contests ban or limit hair extensions for safety reasons. Springy hair noodles, bows, glitter ties, or other hair accessories might be part of your uniform.

Snacks and Stuff

Practices and performances drain moisture from your body. Bring extra water bottles in your pack. A small snack such as fruit helps maintain energy. What else? A camera, small hand towel, and notepad and pencil might come in handy.

Gear Up

You can spend loads of money on cheerleading gear, gadgets, and equipment. Choose wisely. Of all that you can have, your health and your healthy attitude will make the most of your cheerleading experience.

Cheer well!

Hair accessories add the finishing touch.

Further Reading

Cheerleading in Action by John Crossingham.
    Crabtree Publishing Company, New York, New York, 2003.

The Ultimate Guide to Cheerleading
    by Leslie Wilson. Three Rivers Press, New York, New York, 2003.

Edison: Inventing the Century by Neil Baldwin.
    University of Chicago Press, Chicago, Illinois, paperback reprint, 2001.

Web Sites

American Association of Cheerleading Coaches and Advisors
http://www.aacca.org/

CheerHome.com, an online information clearinghouse
http://www.CheerHome.com/

Ms. Pineapple's Cheer Page
http://www.mspineapple.com/

National Cheerleaders Association
http://www.nationalspirit.com/

National Council for Spirit Safety & Education
http://www.spiritsafety.com/

National Federation of State High School Associations
http://www.nfhs.org

United Performing Association, Inc.
http://www.upainc.net/

Universal Cheerleaders Association
http://www.varsity.com

Glossary

amplify (AM pluh FY) — to make louder or greater

anterior cruciate ligament
(an TIR ee ur   KROO shee ATE   LIG uh munt) — a strong band inside the knee that holds the joint steady and connects the thighbone to the shinbone

base (BAYSS) — a cheerleader who steadies the bottom of the stunt and supports the flyer

cardiovascular (KARD ee oh VAS kyoo lur) — the heart and blood, especially as they work with the lungs to supply oxygen to the body

chants (CHANTS) — in cheerleading, the short, repeated singsong phrases often performed on the sidelines in response to big game plays or to fill short pauses in the game action

cheers (CHEERZ) — in cheerleading, the longer phrases that usually rhyme and match with gestures and stunts; cheers distinctly start and end, and often occur during time-outs, halftimes, or other longer game breaks or at competitions

choreography (KOR ee OG ruh fee) — the plan or patterns for dance steps, movement, or action, usually set to music

endurance (en DOOR uhns) — power or strength to keep going or continue for a long time or distance

enthusiasm (en THOO zee AZ um) — excitement or lively interest

flyer (FLIY ur) — a cheerleader who climbs to the top of a stunt and performs an aerial

gesture (JES chur) — hand or arm movement

hamstring (HAM string) — underside of the thigh

icon (EYE kon) — symbol

mascot (MAS kot) — an animal, person, or thing used by a group as its symbol to bring good luck

megaphones (MEG uh FONZ) — cone-shaped devices that direct sound and make it louder

pompon (POM pon) — in cheerleading, the tufted accessory used to add movement, color, and sound to performances; some dictionaries also use pompom or pom-pom

quadriceps (KWOD ruh SEPS) — the large topside muscle of the thigh

rousers (ROUZ urz) — fight songs or school songs

stipends (STY pendz) — payments or allowances

telephonoscope (TEL uh FON uh skope) — a personal hearing aid device invented in 1878 by Thomas Alva Edison (1847-1931) that used two funnels connected by a long tube; a person spoke into one funnel as another person held the other funnel to his ear

tumbling runs (TUM bling RUNZ) — two or more tumbling moves, such as cartwheels or handsprings, performed immediately one after the other

unison (YOO nuh sun) — something done the same way at the same time

ventilation (VENT ul AY shun) — a way to cool or refresh with air

Index

About The Author

Tracy Nelson Maurer specializes in nonfiction and business writing. Her most recently published children's books include the *Roaring Rides* series, also from Rourke Publishing LLC. A former drum majorette and color guard member, Tracy lives near Minneapolis, Minnesota with her husband Mike and their two children.